THE
AMAZING
THINGS
ANIMALS
DO

BY SUSAN McGRATH

BOOKS FOR WORLD EXPLORERS
NATIONAL GEOGRAPHIC SOCIETY

Contents

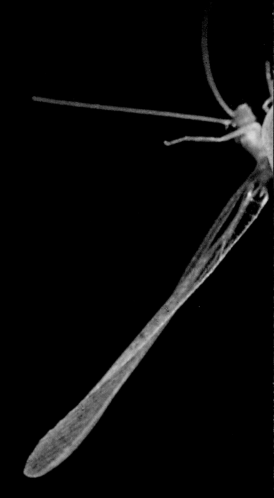

COVER: *Perched on a limb, a cheetah scans the area for a meal. With its lean frame and long legs, it can sprint at amazing speeds—more than 60 miles an hour for short distances. To hunt, it creeps close to an antelope or other prey and quietly watches it. Then WHOOSH! The cat turns on the speed and tries to grab the meal.*
ROBERT CAPUTO

TITLE PAGE: *When is a wreath not a wreath? When it's an armadillo lizard—like this one. In a relaxed position, the South African reptile is long and slender. But when danger threatens, it rolls itself up, gripping the tip of its tail with its mouth. Then its soft belly is protected by its spiky back and tail—its built-in armor.*
© ANTHONY BANNISTER

Copyright © 1989 National Geographic Society
Library of Congress CIP Data: page 96

Loop the Loop!

Aerial acrobat, a green lacewing fly rockets straight up from a leaf, then whips into a backward somersault. To capture three stages of the flip, the photographer made three exposures on one frame. How does a lacewing do its amazing flip? The secret is in the structure of its wings and in the way it controls them. A lacewing has two pairs of wings, which it moves independently. To lift off, then to twirl, it uses the pairs at different times and in different ways. It claps the wings together, then sweeps them up, up, and over its head.

A reader might compare this book to a circus show—with the lacewing's acrobatics as the opening act. The spotlight will shine on five different rings, each with equally amazing performances by animals. In one ring, readers will watch other marvelous movers. In another, they'll see animals that communicate in creative ways. A third ring will feature breathtaking babies. The fourth will have extraordinary eaters. In the fifth ring, animal defenders will demonstrate amazing ways to stay on guard. On with the show!

STEPHEN DALTON/NHPA

1 Motion: It's the Only Way to Go!

An impala explodes into motion, springing 10 feet into the air and hurtling 30 feet forward. Only seconds before, it had been grazing quietly on this African plain. The wind carried the scent of a lion to its keen nostrils—and it leapt into action, racing for safety. Few animals on earth can leap as high and as far as an impala. But other animals move in other amazing ways. Chipmunk-size sugar gliders soar from tree to tree. Lizards called geckoes scale surfaces as slick as glass. Bats zoom through a dark sky, guided by built-in sonar. Turn the pages to meet these and other champions of motion.

S. ROBINSON/NHPA

The klipspringer's balance and coordination rival any circus star's. This small antelope (left) lives in hills and mountains in Africa. From a standing position, it is able to jump three feet or more and can land on an area the size of a silver dollar (above). As it lands, it pulls its feet together. Its rubbery, rounded hooves grip the spot.

With the acceleration of a high-powered sports car, the fastest runner on earth streaks across an African plain (below). To catch prey, a cheetah stalks it, then charges. For a short distance, the cat can sprint at more than 60 miles an hour. The rest of the dash may average 40 miles an hour. If the cheetah has timed its run just right, it will knock down a fleeing antelope in seconds.

Almost all animals move. Kangaroos bounce, frogs hop, snakes slither, horses gallop, and birds fly. Different animals move in different ways, depending on how they are made and where they live. High on a mountain, a klipspringer, a kind of antelope, leaps from rock to rock. On the tips of its small, rounded hooves, it easily lands on steep slopes. Under the ocean, a barnacle, fixed as if with super-glue to a rock, waves armlike tentacles in search of food.

Why do animals move? The question might be compared to the old joke: Why does a chicken cross the road? The chicken crosses for a basic reason: to get to the other side. Likewise, all other animals move for basic reasons—to find food, to avoid danger, and to locate mates. Some move in spectacular ways.

Speed Demons

The cheetah is the fastest mammal on land. For short distances—about the length of 2 football fields—this large African cat can run faster than 60 miles an hour. That means, at full acceleration, a cheetah could be stopped for speeding on many American highways.

The cheetah's body is built for speed. It has a small skull and little fat on its sleek frame. Its legs are long and muscular. Its spine is extremely flexible, curving up and down to help give the cat its extended stride. By holding its strong tail straight behind it, the cheetah balances itself as it rockets over the ground. The tail is used for *(Continued on page 10)*

Herds of wildebeests raise a dust storm galloping across eastern Africa's Serengeti Plain (above). More than a million of the large antelopes migrate together every year. In the dry season, grasses are scarce. The animals may travel 800 miles or more to find food.

High diver, a wildebeest plunges off a bank to cross a river (right). The long trip tests the wildebeest's skill as a swimmer, a runner—and a survivor. If it weakens and slows down, it will be in trouble. Hyenas and other enemies follow the herds, killing those that fall behind.

8

LEN RUE, JR.

More than 100 miles from the Serengeti, wildebeests cross Kenya's Mara River (left). Many more follow them. It may take hours for all the animals to cross. Some grasses grow nearby, but the wildebeests will look for better pastures. How do they know where to go? They watch for storm clouds and listen for thunder. When they detect rain, they head in that direction.

9

JEN AND DES BARTLETT

A male red kangaroo springs along on powerful legs (left). At top speed, it can cover 30 feet with each hop— the length of a large school bus. Kangaroos have been called "living pogo sticks." The diagram shows why. To hop, a kangaroo and a person on a pogo stick both lean forward, then push off. A spring in the pogo stick gives bounce. The kangaroo's feet work like springs.

(Continued from page 7) steering, too. It helps the cat make sudden, sharp turns when chasing prey.

Most of earth's fastest runners have long legs—ostriches, racehorses, and greyhounds, to name a few. But long legs don't necessarily make an animal speedy. An elephant may stand 12 feet tall, but it's no racer. At a weight of more than 6 tons, an elephant has legs as thick as tree trunks. The legs use large amounts of energy just supporting the animal's weight as it stands still. So when the elephant does move, the legs propel it at a lumbering pace that averages from $2\frac{1}{2}$ to 8 miles an hour. Charging, it might go 25 miles an hour. But at its usual pace, it's no faster than the tiny chipmunk. A chipmunk reaches 8 miles an hour on its half-inch-long legs. In fact, it's a speed king among others its size.

Mass Motion

The speedsters are superstars of locomotion, but other animals perform equally impressive feats of endurance and navigation. They migrate hundreds—even thousands—of miles. Animals usually migrate to escape bad conditions, such as cold weather or scarce food, in search of better. Wildebeests are large antelopes that live in southern Africa, where they graze on open plains. During the dry month of May, grasses are scarce. To find food, the animals go north and west—sometimes 800 miles or *(Continued on page 13)*

Creature Feature

Ready . . . set . . . jump! Powered by strong leg muscles, a 2-inch-long grasshopper can jump more than a yard. That's about 20 times the length of its body. With a running start, a young girl, a world champion, covered about 5 yards—slightly more than 3 times her height. If she'd had the muscle power of a grasshopper, she could have jumped more than 25 yards!

BARBARA L. GIBSON

Blast-off! A European tree frog launches itself from a slippery, rain-soaked leaf (left). To capture the action, the photographer made two exposures on one frame. The frog was clinging to the leaf with sticky mucus produced in the soles of its feet. Then it gave a huge push with its muscular hind legs and leapt five feet.

The click beetle jumps without using its legs (above). It makes the move to scare enemies or to turn over if it is stuck on its back. First it arches its body, pulling the tip of its spine into a hook. Then it releases the spine with a loud click, flips into the air, and lands right side up.

11

MICHAEL FOGDEN

Hanging out is what a three-toed sloth and her baby do best (above). A sloth's legs aren't made for standing or walking. Yet they easily hold the sloth as it hangs. Powerful claws grip a branch as the sloth eats, sleeps, mates, and gives birth. Sloths live mainly in South America. Slow movers, they hide from enemies with the help of algae (AL-gee), greenish plant growth that covers their fur and blends with forest colors.

DWIGHT R. KUHN (BOTH)

The gecko is another superclinger. It's a superclimber, too. Its flat toes (bottom, right) are lined with narrow ridges of skin. Tiny hairs grow thickly on the ridges, making them like sticky fingers. The ridges help the gecko grip any dry surface. It can scoot upside down along a branch (top) or ceiling, or scamper up a wall.

12

(Continued from page 10) more. Hundreds of herds travel together. The animals swim rivers and plod across dry plains. Their journey to grassy areas may last several weeks. How do they know which way to go? Studies show that they move in the direction of rain clouds and thunder.

Other migrating animals use other guides. Caribou, sea turtles, and many birds follow positions of the sun and other stars. Pigeons sense and use the earth's magnetic field as a compass. To migrate to their place of birth, Pacific salmon smell and follow chemicals carried from it by water currents.

Scientists are unsure just how monarch butterflies navigate. But they do know that the animals exhibit exceptional qualities of endurance. These fragile orange-and-black insects live in meadows in the northern United States and Canada. Every year, millions of them fly as far as Mexico for the winter. Each weighs about 1/50 of an ounce. They make the 2,000-mile trip south at speeds of more than 20 miles an hour. That's almost as fast as a charging elephant! What's more, pilots have seen the lightweight fliers traveling at altitudes of about 6,000 feet. In spring, the monarchs fly home, and many of them make it. They stop to mate and lay eggs, so the trip takes longer. But it's still a whopping 2,000 miles.

Up... Up...

Not all animals go fast—or far. But they get off the ground in amazing ways. Kangaroos and frogs are expert long jumpers. They'd do well in any track meet. The kangaroo's hindquarters are packed with powerful muscles. To leap, the animal leans forward, balancing with its heavy, muscular tail. Then it springs up on the tips of its toes. Its first leaps may be only a few yards long. But once the animal gets going—sometimes moving 30 miles an hour—it may jump 30 feet in a bound. The tree frog is another leaper. Unlike the kangaroo, it has no tail to steady it as it moves. So the frog relies on its strong, well-coordinated body and limbs. Leaning on its forelimbs, it lifts its hind limbs up on its toes, gives a giant push, and jets into the air.

Then there is the sloth. How it gets off the ground is not as amazing as how it stays off the ground. Sloths are born in trees in South American forests—and spend their lives in

A spider monkey (right) is a real swinger. Such monkeys move through forests of Central and South America by swinging from tree to tree. A prehensile, or grasping, tail helps. The monkey grips a branch with the tail and an arm. Then it pumps itself forward and grabs another branch with its other arm and legs.

the trees. To live in its leafy home, a sloth hangs upside down from branches, using hooklike claws to hold on with a superstrong grip. In that position, the legs hold the sloth as it eats, sleeps, mates, gives birth, and cradles its young. Strong as the legs are, they could never keep up with those of a kangaroo, a frog—or even a creeping turtle. The legs don't support weight on the ground. If a sloth climbs or tumbles down—which is rare—it drags itself along on its belly. In water, it swims quickly. But on the ground or above it, the sloth is one of earth's slowest mammals. To go the length of a branch, it moves foreleg over foreleg and hind leg over hind leg. With rest stops, the trip may take hours.

...And Away!

Getting out of the trees and into the air calls for another kind of motion: flight. Birds, bats, and some insects are the only animals that actually fly. Other animals, however, come close. One is the sugar glider, a mammal that grows to about the size of a chipmunk. It lives in forests of Australia and New Guinea, where it glides from tree to tree. The glider uses winglike flaps of skin that connect its forelegs and hind legs. To set sail, it dives from a high branch. Then it holds out its legs and stretches its body flat. Like a furry paper airplane, the glider may soar 150 *(Continued on page 17)*

C. & S. POLLITT/AUSTRALASIAN NATURE TRANSPARENCIES

Hang glider of the animal world, an adult sugar glider (left), slightly larger than a chipmunk, soars through a forest in Australia. A glider is born with its gear. Loose skin connects its forelegs and hind legs. As it dives from a branch, it flattens out and extends its legs, becoming a kind of kite. It may glide 150 feet to another branch.

*Lift-off! From a treetop, this sifaka (suh-FAHK-uh)
pushed off with powerful hind legs. To prepare for
landing, it spreads all its limbs. It can sail 30 feet to
another tree. Unlike the glider, which soars downward
headfirst, the sifaka leaps upright. Related to monkeys,
sifakas live on Africa's island of Madagascar.*

Winging it, a bat speeds through the dark (above). Bats are the only mammals that fly. Their wings are skin-covered extensions of their forelimbs. To fly at night, bats use a system called echolocation. A bat makes rapid clicks in its throat. The sounds bounce off obstacles in its path. The echo helps guide the bat.

(Continued from page 14) feet. When it reaches a lower branch, it pulls in its hind legs and lands on all fours.

In terms of speed, the sugar glider can't compete with most winged animals—especially birds called swifts. In fact, not even a cheetah could keep up with a large swift. About the size of an American robin, the bird can zoom through the air faster than 100 miles an hour.

Birds in general move faster than any other kind of animal. Here's why. Most birds have low body weight and high strength. Their feathers and bones are hollow. They have light beaks in place of heavy teeth. And they lay eggs in a nest. This means they don't carry heavy young in their bodies, as mammals do. Swifts are more streamlined than other birds. They have short legs and small feet. In flight, a swift tucks them close to its body. At rest, it hooks its strong claws into bark or a rock crevice and hangs upside down. But a swift rarely rests. It may dart about all day catching insects.

Going fast forward in the air is one feat. Maneuvering in the air is another. In that department, the acrobatic hummingbird outclasses all other birds. Called the helicopter of the bird world, the tiny hummer can hover motionless in the air, fly straight up with its body vertical, and even scoot backward. The secret of the hummer's flexible flying is in its wings. The wings of birds have joints much like a human's elbows and wrists. When most birds flap their wings, the

Tiny but talented, a hummingbird (right) hovers at a flower. It can outmaneuver bigger birds just as a helicopter outmaneuvers an airplane. The wings of a hummingbird are strong and rigid. By moving them in a figure-eight pattern, the bird hovers, zooms forward, and even rockets straight up.

wings bend. A hummingbird's joints are rigid, so its wings go up and down like oars. To hover, it moves the stiff wings back and forth in a figure-eight pattern, making about 3,000 figure eights a minute. This creates a hum, like the buzz of a bee. Swivel joints at the shoulders allow the bird to tilt its wings to different angles. Depending on the angle, the hummer flies forward, backward, or up and down.

In the Swim

Water opens up another world of motion. Many animals move easily in the water, even if they're heavy. The blue whale, a mammal, weighs 30 times more than an adult elephant. But it moves more gracefully—and usually faster—than the elephant does. The whale is fully supported by water, so it doesn't burn up energy just resting. It has plenty of energy for swimming. It strokes its huge, horizontal tail flukes up and down, pushing itself forward up to 25 miles an hour. It balances and steers with flippers at its sides. It even twirls and turns with such skill that some call it a dancer.

Fish use their tails for swimming, too. But most fish move their tails from side to side, rather than up and down. With this motion, some fish can outswim a whale. The tuna, a large ocean fish, can reach speeds of 43 miles an hour.

Not all marine animals swim to get around. The octopus sometimes uses jet propulsion. An octopus has a soft, baglike body composed of muscle. While it is moving, the animal gently contracts and relaxes its body, sending water in and out of its body cavity. When threatened, the octopus contracts the muscle with great force. Water blasts out of a tube, shooting the octopus forward.

In the animal world, ways of getting around are about as varied as the ways people get around on land, in the water, or through the skies. Whatever the method, one thing stays the same: Motion is the only way to go!

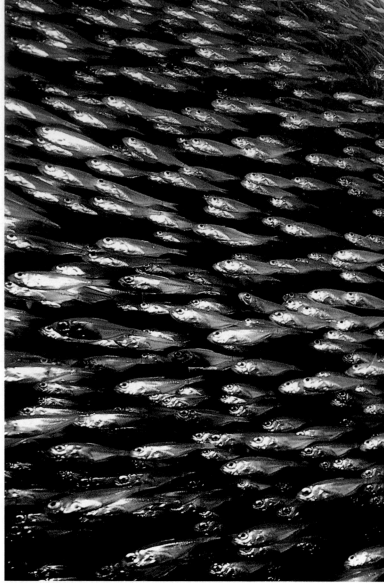

Thousands of fish sweep through the ocean in a glittery school (above). No one is sure why fish form schools. Some scientists think the grouping reduces water resistance, speeding up the school's search for food and its escape from enemies. Others think a school discourages enemies. As the fish crowd together, the enemy can't concentrate on just one—so it may give up.

An octopus in a hurry (left) hurtles past a sea anenome (uh-NEM-uh-nee). To travel at top speed, an octopus doesn't use its eight arms. It sucks water into a hollow sac in its body, then blasts it out through a tube called a siphon. The water shoots in one direction, and the octopus jets away in the other.

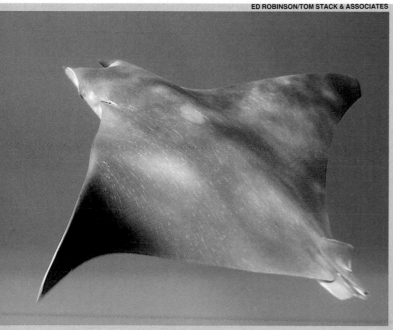

Resembling a gigantic prehistoric bird, a manta ray "flies" along the sea bottom (left). The ray measures 20 feet across and weighs $1\frac{1}{2}$ tons. To swim, it flaps its winglike fins (above). The fins slowly move up and down in powerful, rippling strokes. The rolling motion comes from the manta's flexible frame. It is not made of bone, but of a softer material called cartilage.

LOIS SLOAN

Adélie (uh-DAY-lee) penguins head for Antarctic waters. Diving, the birds may be airborne for an instant. But they never actually fly. Their stiff wings are too small. The wings, however, work as flippers in the water. They help propel a penguin as fast as 37 miles an hour. On ice, penguins waddle or slide on their bellies.

ART WOLFE

2
Do Tell!

S-T-R-E-T-C-H! A male hippopotamus packs a powerful yawn. His mouth opens so wide that his jaws nearly form a vertical line. Each front tooth extends 20 inches and weighs several pounds. Actually, this isn't a yawn at all. It's the beginning of a threat display—the hippo's way of communicating with another male hippo that has trespassed on his territory. First, he shows the huge teeth. Then he lets out a thunderous roar, rears up on his hind legs, and splashes down. If the intruder wants to avoid a fight, he will crouch or run. This shows that he accepts this hippo's claim to the area. The hippo is just one creature that communicates in amazing ways. Meet other creative communicators on the next pages.

LEN RUE, JR.

JEFF FOOTT

Two black-tailed prairie dogs greet (above), sniffing and nuzzling. By "kissing," they recognize each other's scent and can tell that they share the same part of a town. Prairie dogs are social animals. They lie together and groom each other's fur with their paws and teeth. This cozy behavior strengthens bonds between them.

Like prairie dogs, wolves (below) are social animals. Communications between wolves are complex. Here, two males struggle to prove which is the stronger, or dominant, wolf. Soon, one will back down and slink away to show that he is no longer a threat. The dominant wolf will stand and survey his territory.

C. ALLAN MORGAN

In the animal kindgom, there are plenty of things to say and plenty of ways to say them. Every animal species has its own distinctive ways of giving messages to other animals. Each has particular ways of using sight, sound, scent, and touch to form the messages. Two prairie dogs touch noses and sniff each other to say "I recognize you." A chimp barks softly to say "Stay away!" Animals communicate to find mates, to warn others of danger, to identify their young, to announce their presence to rivals, to avoid crowding, and just to get along well together.

Making Sense

Many animals in this book are social animals—animals that live in groups. Social animals share food and activities, and so they must constantly communicate. Generally, they use their senses. Different senses are often used to communicate different things.

A wolf pack is one kind of social group. The pack usually has eight or more members and is organized much like a royal court. In a court, a king and queen have the highest rank. Below them come princes and princesses, and so on. In a pack, the leader is called the alpha male. All other males rank at various lower levels. The females have similar rankings of their own.

To communicate his dominance within the pack, the alpha male used a touch message: He struggled with other

WOLFGANG BAYER

A baboon picks through a companion's fur (above), plucking out bits of dirt, parasites, and flakes of dead skin. The monkey's touch is soothing and feels good. It communicates warm feelings between the baboons.

HUGO VAN LAWICK

LOIS SLOAN

Let's face it. This could be a chimpanzee's motto. With facial muscles as flexible as a human's, the chimp—an ape—uses many different expressions when communicating with other chimps. The chimp in the photograph pulls back its lips, showing fear. From left to right in the diagram, it rounds its mouth in a greeting pout; it presses together its lips and frowns in a threat display; and it relaxes its face at play to say, "I'm having fun."

Center of attention, a worker honeybee does a waggle dance in her hive (diagram below). Other workers, always female, gather round. The dance tells them how to find flowers she has just visited. Her steps tell where the flowers are. Sacs on her legs hold pollen. Its odor reveals the type of flowers. She may even share tastes of nectar. Later, the bees will buzz right to the flowers.

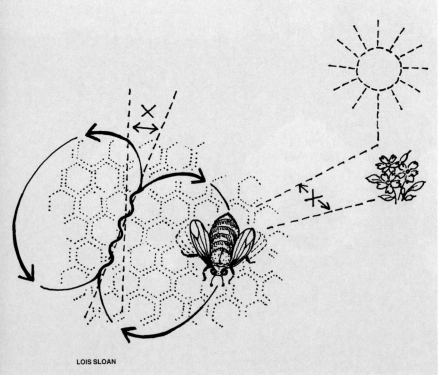

males. Next, he used a scent message to mark the pack's territory against intruders: He sprayed his urine on trees and rocks. Now, each time the alpha male meets other pack members, he uses sight messages to reinforce his rank: He holds his head high and his tail straight up. "I'm in charge," his posture shows. The others crouch and tuck their tails between their legs. "I'm no threat," their posture answers.

Vocal messages play a major part in the pack's daily life. Wolves are members of the dog family, so they whine, growl, or yelp, depending on what they want to communicate. Before hunting, a pack usually gathers and lets out a group howl—in eerie harmony. No one is sure why wolves give a group howl. The howl may promote unity, helping the pack hunt well together; it may announce the pack's location to other packs; or it may help a stray wolf find its pack.

Touching Base

Wolves are top-notch communicators in every sense. Many social animals, however, communicate best by staying in touch—literally. They may groom each other as a way of lowering tension and strengthening ties within a group. Apes, for example, pick through one another's fur with their fingers. Monkeys follow a like routine. They clean out parasites, dead skin, and dirt. This may seem to be an odd sort of communication, but scientists think grooming conveys a strong message: "I like you. We have a good relationship."

Touch can be a touchy subject when animals are establishing dominance or territorial rights, or when they are trying to win mates. Then, males may fight. Klipspringers use their short, pointed horns for jabbing. Baboons use their sharp front teeth for slashing. Elephants use their tusks as battering rams against each other. Mock fights often take the place of real fights. The animals touch, but neither is really hurt. Two male giraffes, for instance, stand stiff-legged, side by side. Their long necks wind around each other in snakelike fashion. They shove and butt one another with their heads. The giraffes are performing a mock fight called "necking." The action (Continued on page 30)

Do the Waggle! A honeybee waggle dances (left) to help other bees find flowers more than 250 feet away. On honeycomb, the bee moves in a figure eight. The angle X at which she traces the eight equals the angle X between the sun and the flowers. This information gives the position of the flowers. In the center of the eight, the bee waggles, or vibrates, her body. The time of the waggle gives the flowers' distance from the hive.

A young male giraffe stands firm as another pushes him with his head and neck (right). The giraffes shove and butt to establish which is dominant. They learned such communication from adults. Later, they will use it to fight for a mate. Here, neither animal really gets hurt.

Sometimes an animal challenges another's message. Then the two may fight. Here, a male springbok has challenged another's claim to territory in Africa by straying inside boundaries marked with the other's droppings. The defending male attacks the intruder. The fight will end when one animal, perhaps hurt, flees.

CHARLES G. SUMMERS, JR.

FRANS LANTING

Sitting pretty, a male frigatebird in the Galápagos Islands displays his red throat pouch (above). A male may puff up his pouch until it is almost the size of a soccer ball. Then he will throw back his head, cry out, and shake his wings. The show asks females to choose him as a mate, and it tells other males to stay away.

Hey! Over here! A male fiddler crab (right) waves his huge claw to attract a female of his species. In each species, the claw is a different color and is waved in a different pattern. This crab waves his white claw up and down to call a mate. Only males have one big claw. The other claw is small and scoops up food.

(Continued from page 26) establishes which male is stronger. The dominant one will mate with a female.

Some animals resolve differences without touching at all. They communicate through the sense of sight. Like hippos, some might defend territory by showing off weapons such as teeth or antlers. Others might raise their fur to appear bigger than they are. Still others might charge at full speed. Often the challenger will back down and slink away.

Seeing is Believing

In some cases, sight messages are an animal's best—or only—means of communication. Fireflies flashing in the dark are saying much more than: "Summer is here." They are sending messages to one another. A male firefly of a particular species flashes in a fixed pattern. He might make two flashes every two seconds. The flashes mean: "I am a male." A female of the same species might respond by flashing her light once for each pair of flashes he gives off. She says: "I am a female, and I am over here." Then the male flies to her, and they mate.

Visual signals have the advantage of speed, but they have disadvantages, too. Sights can't travel around obstacles. Except for a firefly's flashing light, visual signals usually can't be seen at night. Because of these drawbacks, communications that must be seen are best used in closeup situations. For example, many male birds perform elaborate visual rituals during courtship. Sometimes they use brightly colored feathers or other built-in finery. When a peacock wants to attract a female, a peahen, he spreads his dazzling green-and-blue tail feathers into a fan and struts before her.

The male frigatebird, a large black seabird found on tropical islands, has a pouch under his bill. For most of the

DIETER AND MARY PLAGE/BRUCE COLEMAN LTD.

One and two and. . . . Laysan albatrosses perform a step in a ritual courtship dance (left). Scientists count about eight different steps. First, the male faces the female and opens his bill. Next, the birds nibble bills (left in diagram). In a final step, both raise their bills to the sky and cry out—a move called skypointing (right).

LOIS SLOAN

A male Caspian tern brings a gift of fish to a female (above). This is how he asks her to become his mate. By giving her food, the male shows her that he will be a good provider. He also helps nourish her so that she can produce eggs. If the female accepts his offer, the terns may mate for life. Then the pair will repeat this courtship behavior every breeding season. Such communication helps strengthen their relationship.

year, the pouch is barely visible. But during mating season, the bird inflates it into a red balloon. To attract a female, he throws back his head and wings, showing off the pouch. At the same time, he shakes his wings and calls out.

Blue-footed boobies, another kind of seabird, have bright blue feet. The feet play a part in the birds' highly visual courtship ritual. First, the male parades before the female, showing off his feet. If interested, the female parades, too. Next, both birds throw back their heads, point their bills and wings to the sky, and cry out. The gesture is called sky-pointing. Then one may pick up a twig and put it down as if to begin building a nest. Before mating, they may offer gifts of sticks to one another and gently touch bills.

Black-and-white seabirds called albatrosses perform a similar courtship ritual. It's not as colorful—but it's just as successful. Colorful or not, visual signals help birds of a feather flock together.

Something in the Air

Signals carried in scents don't travel at the speed of light, as visual signals do. But a scent message can be left to work long after the communicator has moved on. So scent is a useful way of marking territorial boundaries. A hippo or a rhinoceros leaves droppings as a marker. A klipspringer marks trees with a scented liquid from a facial gland. A cheetah sprays urine to mark its area. Scent signals also help animals recognize their young. After a sea lion mother gives birth to a pup, she licks it clean. Then she sniffs its breath and body scent. She will *(Continued on page 35)*

DWIGHT R. KUHN

Tuning in, a male luna moth (above) adjusts his feathery antennae. They help him locate a female of his species. When a female is ready to mate, her glands release a scent called a pheromone. The male picks up the scent with his antennae, then follows it to her.

PAUL STERRY/NATURE PHOTOGRAPHERS LTD.

After flying a mile over wooded terrain, a male emperor moth perches below a female on a bush (left). He found her by following her pheromone trail. She gave off just a puff of the scent. The male's antennae are so sensitive that they can detect the scent from far away.

Scratch and sniff. A male klipspringer (right) rubs liquid from a gland on his face onto a twig. The liquid is scented. The smell tells other males that this is part of his territory. If the other males ignore the warning and trespass, they may find themselves in for a fight.

A male king cheetah (below) backs up to a tree and sprays urine on it to mark his territory. The urine contains chemicals that other cheetahs recognize by smell. Such a signal has an advantage over a visual signal. Like a written message, scent lingers after the communicator has gone. Scent marking is ideal communication for animals that claim big spaces.

(Continued from page 32) depend on memory to recognize the pup by its scent, even after it is grown.

Moths use scent messages to attract mates. A female has glands on her abdomen that hold a chemical called a pheromone (FER-uh-mone). To moths, pheromones have a strong smell. During mating season, the female releases a pheromone. Wind may spread the scent for more than a mile. A male picks up the scent with his feathery antennae and follows it to her. Scents from many different species may fill the air. The male's antennae are especially fine-tuned to detect the scent of females of his own species.

Sounds of Music

Sound has many advantages in communication. For one thing, sound travels a long way. So animals don't need to see each other to communicate. Sounds can carry a lot of information, too.

The pitch and length of a ground squirrel's warning cry tell other ground squirrels whether an approaching predator is a bird, such as a hawk, or a tunneling animal, such as a badger. This is important information. To escape a hawk, the squirrel can duck into any burrow entrance. Escaping a badger isn't so easy. When a ground squirrel hears that alert, it tries to scoot deep inside a burrow—preferably one with an opening for escape at the other end.

Many animals use song to communicate. Howler monkeys are treetop vocalists that live in the forests of South America. A howler has a huge sac on its throat that amplifies its voice. The animal inflates the sac, then calls out. The resulting howl carries through the forest. Group howls help keep a troop of the monkeys together. The howls also tell other troops that the area is occupied.

Howler monkeys aren't the only animals that use amplifiers. Some male frogs inflate sacs on their throats to call mates. The sacs make their croaks extra loud. Elephant seals were named for the amplifiers the males have— trunklike noses 15 inches long. In mating season, a male bellows through his nose. The blast warns rivals that the surrounding beach—and the females on it—belong to him.

One of the most complex sounds in the animal kingdom is the song of the humpback whale. Scientists have learned

Here I am! The loud, abrupt call of a male Victoria riflebird (left) seems to say just that. This Australian bird uses the call to attract mates and to claim his territory. His colorful throat and feathers reinforce the messages. To get a point across, animals often use more than one form of communication. Like this bird, they may call out and show off at the same time.

HANS AND JUDY BESTE

RAT-A-TAT! A great spotted woodpecker (below) beats drumrolls on a dead tree. The tree is hollow and amplifies the pecking sound. The length of the rolls and the pauses between them tell other woodpeckers that this bird is of the great spotted species. Other species identify themselves by drumming different patterns.

W.S. PATON/NATURE PHOTOGRAPHERS LTD.

that all male humpbacks in one area sing the same song, usually during mating season. But scientists are not sure what the song means. Like a human song, the whale song has verses. The whales repeat the verses over and over again, in the same order. Each season, the song changes slightly. Old verses are dropped and new ones are added. The music may travel more than 750 miles through the water and may go on for hours at a time. One scientist finally gave up recording one whale's song after 22 straight hours.

Not all animals manufacture sounds with a voice. Rabbits thump their feet on the ground to say that an enemy is near. Beavers smack their tails on the surface of the water to warn other beavers of a predator. To attract mates, grasshoppers chirp by rubbing a hind leg against a projection on one wing. If alarmed, a trumpeter swan not only calls out but also extends its snow-white wings to a span of eight feet. It beats them rapidly, creating a loud rushing sound. Then it takes off. Others in its flock follow in graceful flight, leaving a startled enemy behind. Communication works!

C. ALLAN MORGAN

Four-ton heavyweights, male northern elephant seals (above) rear up and roar. The sound carries for miles. It's mating season, and the two are fighting to control part of a beach in Mexico. Females have gathered there. The winning male will mate with them for the next three months. He will guard them closely, not even leaving to find food. His body fat will nourish him.

Calling all females! With the help of a vocal sac on his throat, a tiny male grey tree frog (left) broadcasts his message loud and clear. He amplifies his voice by inflating the sac at the same time he creates sound in his throat. During mating season, males may gather to croak in a chorus of thousands.

Creature Feature

BARBARA L. GIBSON

POP . . . POP . . . Coffee perking? Popcorn popping? Neither. Each spring, male sage grouse on plains in western North America (above) compete for places on display grounds. All try to win spots at the center of the grounds. That's where females look for mates. While competing, the males whistle and make loud popping noises: They inflate sacs on their chests, then quickly deflate them. The sounds boom across the plains.

Baby on board, a howler monkey mother (left) lets out a protective roar. Nearby, other howlers in her troop join in. A troop howls together at least once a day. By puffing up their throat pouches, howlers amplify their voices. A group howl may ring for a mile through South American forests. Many troops share a forest, yet they rarely meet. Howling tells other troops to stay away.

Swimming near the Bahamas, Atlantic spotted dolphins let out a stream of clicks and whistles. The clicks hit obstacles and bounce back to the mammals, helping guide them. Dolphins whistle to cooperate in finding food and to warn each other of danger. A dolphin may whistle if it is sick or injured. Then the others may push it to the surface to help it breathe.

HOWARD HALL

3
Bringing Up Baby

Thanks, Mom. After drinking its mother's milk, a young African elephant caresses her mouth with its trunk. The 250-pound baby mammal drinks several gallons of milk a day. Before giving birth, the mother carried the developing baby inside her for nearly 2 years. Now she will nurse the youngster until it is 3 years old. Across the globe in Alaska, a salmon lays 8,000 eggs in a stream, then leaves them to hatch on their own. Only a few babies survive. In terms of child care, the elephant and the salmon are at two extremes. Read on to see how others bring up babies.

STAN OSOLINSKI

A baby giraffe (above) is a born traveler. Its mother gives birth standing up, so its first trip is a five-foot drop to the ground. The baby is relaxed and is not hurt.

About half an hour later, it stands up. Within ten hours, it runs beside its mother, with the herd. In no time, it moves fast enough to flee lions and other enemies.

A re the following statements true or false? All mammals give birth to live, miniature versions of themselves. All other animals lay eggs.

Neither statement is entirely true—or false. *Most* mammals do give birth to live young. *Most* other animals do lay eggs. But some animals are in categories all their own. They give birth in ways that depart from the usual.

Take the case of mammals called monotremes. They're mammals that lay eggs. The Australian platypus and the echidna (ih-KID-nah), or spiny anteater, are the only monotremes. A platypus mother lays one or two soft-shell eggs in a deep, underground burrow. She curls her tail around the eggs to keep them warm until they hatch about ten days later. Then she nurses the young with milk from her body for several months until they can live on their own.

An echidna is covered with sharp spines. The female lays a single egg into a shallow pouch on her belly. After the young hatches, it lives and nurses in the pouch until its own spines start to grow—at about eight weeks. To avoid a prickly situation, the mother quickly puts it out, into a hidden nest. From there, the baby echidna (Continued on page 46)

Break time. A kangaroo and her baby, a joey, pause between hops (right). Kangaroos are mammals called marsupials. The mother carries her young in a pouch on her belly. Born blind and hairless, a joey is the size of a lima bean. After birth, it crawls into the pouch, clings to a nipple, and begins nursing. It feeds and develops inside the pouch for about eight months.

JOHN CANCALOSI

KATHIE ATKINSON/OXFORD SCIENTIFIC FILMS

The echidna (left), found in Australia and New Guinea, is a mammal called a monotreme. Female monotremes give birth by laying eggs. An echidna egg hatches inside the mother's stomach pouch (below). The baby stays in the pouch until its spines grow. Then out it goes.

LOIS SLOAN

DWIGHT R. KUHN

An insect called an aphid (above) gives birth to live young—without mating. She makes copies of herself. The process is triggered when food is plentiful, from spring through fall. Then, she produces females and males. Later, her offspring mate, and the females lay eggs. These hatch in spring, and the cycle begins again.

A baby brittle star, a sea creature, pulls itself out of its mother's body (below). There are many kinds of brittle stars. In this case, the mother carries and hatches one to three eggs inside her. Later, the young crawl out, arm over arm. Other mothers reproduce by releasing eggs, which the male then fertilizes.

© ANTHONY BANNISTER

PAUL STERRY/NATURE PHOTOGRAPHERS LTD.

Its 12 tentacles wrapped in a ball, a light-colored baby sea anemone floats out of its mother (above). It will open the tentacles, then drift off. Later, it will cling to a rock and grow into an adult. The mother carried the developing baby inside her. Other kinds of anemones, both male and female, reproduce by splitting in two.

This odd-looking "baby" (left) is a new sea star. It was "born" through regeneration. An adult sea star lost one of its five arms. Then the arm slowly grew four smaller ones. In about a year, these new arms will be as long as the original one. The adult that lost the arm will replace it at the same rate.

2

3

1

(Continued from page 43) pokes its head inside the mother's pouch to nurse. At six months, it is on its own.

Insects usually only lay eggs. The plant-sucking aphid is an exception. One generation of females mates and lays eggs. The next generation produces live young, without mating. Here's how the cycle works: Male and female aphids mate in late fall. The females lay eggs. In spring, the eggs produce females only. Through summer, a young female may give birth to 200 live females. In early fall, she produces live males. She does both without mating. Scientists think such births are triggered by abundant food in warm months. By reproducing, the female uses the supply. In late fall her offspring mate, beginning a new cycle.

Double Duty

Sea animals called corals have two ways of reproducing. Among some kinds, the female releases eggs and the male fertilizes them. The eggs develop into small, swimming creatures. These attach themselves to a hard surface and grow into adults. Among other kinds, each adult divides into two complete corals. Billions of these corals pile up, creating a huge structure—a reef.

In the case of sea stars, some kinds might be called double trouble. The female always reproduces by laying eggs, which the male then fertilizes. But both males and females also reproduce in another, more amazing way— one that confused fishermen for years. Many fishermen think of sea stars as pests. The creatures eat fish, reducing the supply. At sea, fishermen used to break up sea stars and throw them overboard—that is, until they found out that some kinds can reproduce through *(Continued on page 50)*

① *A female cicada lays an egg in a slit in a twig. Cicadas might be called Rip Van Winkles of the insect world. A cicada's life cycle includes a nap that may be 2, 5, 13, or 17 years long. This kind takes a 13-year nap. Its cycle begins in spring, as adults mate and lay eggs.*

② *In 6 weeks, an ant-size cicada, or nymph, emerges from an egg. The nymph drops to the ground, burrows in, and lives there, sucking root sap. After 13 years, it digs out and climbs a tree—shown here.*

③ *Soon a full-grown adult bursts from the nymph skin through a crack on the back. No one knows why cicadas come out at such long and varied intervals. They mate, lay eggs, then die. In time, their young will do the same.*

In the swim, tiny baby sea horses tumble from a pouch in their father's body (right). The pouch still bulges with more babies. Male sea horses are among the few fathers that help care for developing young. A female lays eggs in a male's pouch. He fertilizes and holds them. A week after they hatch, he lets the babies out.

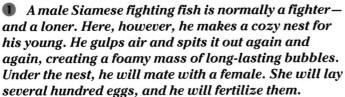

① *A male Siamese fighting fish is normally a fighter—and a loner. Here, however, he makes a cozy nest for his young. He gulps air and spits it out again and again, creating a foamy mass of long-lasting bubbles. Under the nest, he will mate with a female. She will lay several hundred eggs, and he will fertilize them.*

② *The male scoops up the eggs in his mouth and spits them into the nest. Once he has stored them all, he will become very protective and will chase the female away.*

③ *The eggs lie safely in the bubble nest, guarded by their father. He often repairs the nest, adding new bubbles. In about a week, the eggs will hatch, and the babies will huddle under the nest. If one slips away, the father will gently return it to the nest in his mouth. Soon the nest will break up, and the young will depart. The father's parental instincts will depart, too. He will ignore the young—and may even eat some of them.*

Creature Feature

Upside down is a cozy position for a newborn flying fox—a kind of bat. Its mother cradles it in her wings. Right after birth, a flying fox clings to its mother's body with its feet and thumbs. Then, guided by one of her wings, the baby crawls down to her chest. If the baby loses its grip and starts to fall, mother comes to the rescue. She wraps the wing around it.

BARBARA L. GIBSON

49

(Continued from page 46) regeneration. Even a sea star arm stays alive. Slowly, the arm grows new limbs to replace the missing ones. By breaking up the sea stars, fishermen were actually adding thousands to the sea!

Animals such as corals, aphids, and sea stars don't need a lot of tender loving care from parents. But many other animals do. In most species, the mother takes charge of raising the young. A kangaroo mother, for instance, nurses and guards her baby in her pouch for about eight months. Elephant mothers take turns watching their babies in a group scientists call a kindergarten. In other species, male and female work together. Albatross parents take turns incubating eggs. Beaver mates both watch out for their kits.

Bye-bye, Baby

In some species, it's father that seems to know best. A male sea horse is one such father. The female lays eggs in a pouch on his belly—sometimes 250 eggs at once. There he keeps them safe as they develop. A week after the babies hatch, he opens a slit on the front, and out they pop. Sea horses don't feed or guard their young. Once the babies are out of the pouch, father's duty is done.

European cuckoos don't take care of their babies at all. A female lays her eggs in the nests of other kinds of birds that have flown off for a while. In a season, she may lay ten or more eggs in different nests. She usually chooses nests with eggs similar in color and shape to hers. The cuckoo's eggs may be larger, but the nest owners don't see a difference and incubate her eggs with theirs.

A cuckoo baby is trouble from the start. After hatching, it pushes the other eggs and babies out of the nest. It constantly screeches for food, exhausting the foster parents. Finally, it may grow to twice the size of these parents. As an adult, a female cuckoo will repeat her mother's tricks. Although a cuckoo's means of child care may be inconvenient for other birds, it's efficient for the cuckoo. Without responsibility as a parent, the cuckoo gets a head start on its migration south. It enjoys a longer period of warm weather—and it avoids the hard work of bringing up baby!

1 One egg in this nest is different from the others. But the nest owner, a sparrow-size bird called a dunnock, hasn't noticed. She laid four eggs, then flew off to find food. While she was gone, a female European cuckoo ate a dunnock egg and replaced it with one of her own.

2 The cuckoo chick hatches before most of the others.

3 It shoves the dunnock eggs and a chick out of the nest. Now it can have all the dunnock mother's care.

4 The growing cuckoo soon makes a midget out of the dunnock. It cries constantly for food, tiring the small mother. Nearby, the cuckoo mother may be resting. She lays about ten eggs a year. But by tricking other birds into raising the young, she never lifts a wing.

A king penguin rolls its egg up onto its feet and tucks it under a fold of skin on its belly. For 52 days, the parents will take turns incubating the egg this way. They can even waddle while holding it. When the egg hatches, they will care for the chick for up to a year. The attention helps increase the baby's chance of survival.

FRANCISCO ERIZE/BRUCE COLEMAN LTD.

4
Back to Basics

ZAP! A chameleon's tongue shoots out to grab a grasshopper. Between meals, the six-inch-long tongue folds neatly in the lizard's mouth. When the chameleon spies food, the tongue jets forward. A sticky bulb at the tip snags the prey. The chameleon is just one animal that performs a basic function of life—eating, drinking, or breathing—in an amazing way. A flamingo eats with its bill upside down. Some kinds of fish can climb on land and breathe air. Turn the page for more.

FRANS LANTING

When it comes to eating, most animals have particular tastes. The gerenuk (GER-uh-nook), for instance, is an herbivore, or plant-eater—and it doesn't eat just any plants. This African antelope dines on tree shoots and leaves. It often balances on its hind legs, its forelegs propped against a branch 6 feet high. A giraffe, with its long neck and legs, feeds higher still—on leaves 17 feet above the ground. A tiny African dik-dik, a kind of antelope, eats low-growing shrubs. A Thomson's gazelle eats grass from the floor of an African plain. Herbivores generally have an easy time finding food—it grows all around them. Carnivores, animals that eat meat, usually work harder for meals.

A leopard is one carnivore that catches most of its food. This powerful African cat uses strength and skill. It singles out an animal and creeps toward it on great, padded paws. Within striking distance, it rockets forward and pounces on its prey. The cat can't relax yet. With hyenas and other hungry rivals around, it must guard its catch. It hauls the prey up a tree, then eats it there, returning often to finish it.

Other hunters have different ways of keeping a hard-earned meal all to themselves. A (Continued on page 59)

PETER JOHNSON/NHPA

Leftovers again! A leopard looks down from a tree where it has draped its prey (above). The powerful cat can drag a dead animal heavier than itself up into high branches. Many other animals looking for a free meal would like to share this one. That's why the leopard is careful to hide its catch up high.

ANIMALS ANIMALS/BRUCE DAVIDSON

A gerenuk (left) balances on its hind legs to nibble leaves of an acacia tree. The long-necked African antelope can stand on two legs for hours, moving around a tree to feed. Its diet of leaves enables the gerenuk to live in areas too dry for grasses to grow.

56

For breakfast, an African egg-eating snake (below) likes its egg raw—shell included. This egg is many times larger than the snake's head. But loose hinges connecting the snake's jaws allow it to open its mouth extra wide. The whole egg fits right in. As the snake swallows (below, right), its muscles squeeze the egg against its spine, crushing the egg. The snake will gulp down the egg's insides, then spit out the shell.

MICHAEL FOGDEN (BOTH)

(Continued from page 56) wolf can "wolf down" 20 pounds of meat at once. In a day, a lion can eat 60 pounds.

Owls don't waste time picking through a carcass for the edible bits. They devour their prey whole, then bring up the bones and other indigestible parts later.

Most owls are night hunters. With their keen night vision—many times sharper than a human's—they wing through the dark, easily avoiding obstacles. Extra-sensitive ears help an owl hunt. With them, the owl detects the slightest rustling of a mouse or beetle on the ground. Then the bird swoops with claws outstretched and snatches the prey.

Going Fishing

Compared with the owl's smooth swoop, the brown pelican's crash dive might seem clumsy. This pelican, however, is just as skilled a hunter as is the owl. A seabird, the brown pelican goes after fish. It flies over the water, constantly scouting for the prey. When it spots a fish, it folds its wings back and dives. It plunges into the water and scoops up the fish in its large, pouched bill. Then the bird surfaces, drains the water from its bill, and swallows the catch.

Underwater, a slender, striped fish is also fishing—but in a very different way. Beside a reef, it wags its body up and down, attracting attention. A larger fish approaches, mouth open. Suddenly, the small fish darts into the other's mouth. The small fish has a purpose. It's a (Continued on page 62)

Silent hunter, an eastern screech-owl returns to its nest with a caterpillar (left). Keen eyes and ears help the owl detect the faintest rustling on the ground. Then it silently snatches up prey. Its feathers have soft, fringed edges that ease airflow during flight—and limit noise.

JOHN F. O'CONNOR: PHOTO/NATS

A double-exposure photograph of a saw-whet owl facing right (below) shows why the bird doesn't need eyes in the back of its head for hunting. A flexible neck lets it turn its head 180° and see directly behind it. Fine hearing helps the owl locate food. Stiff feathers around its face capture sound and channel it to the owl's ears.

DWIGHT R. KUHN

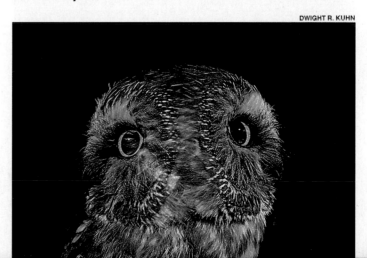

JEFF FOOTT

Brown pelicans (above) angle their wings back and plunge after fish. Each dives for a fish it has spotted from above. It traps the fish—and up to three gallons of water—in its bill. Before eating its catch, a pelican bows its head and drains the water. Then it tosses its head back and swallows its meal . . .

FRITZ PÖLKING

. . . unless a pirate—like this frigatebird (above)— grabs the food first. A frigatebird often gets fish by snatching it from other birds, such as this young pelican. A frigatebird's feathers aren't completely waterproof, so it can't dive for its own fish.

WILLIAM BOEHM/WEST STOCK

Alaskan fisher, a brown bear (above) wades to shore with its catch—a plump salmon—in its mouth. It snagged the fish with its sharp claws and teeth. Brown bears eat many foods, such as nuts, berries, and insects. But in late summer, salmon is their favorite

meal. Then, thousands of the fish swim upstream through Alaskan waters to lay eggs. Many brown bears may gather at a good fishing hole, including mothers teaching their cubs how to fish.

(Continued from page 59) cleaner wrasse (RASS) going after a meal. A wrasse eats pests that live on other fish. Its color and movements announce that it offers valuable cleaning services. Other fish allow the wrasse to groom them, without harming it. The wrasse might be called a doctor. It helps maintain the health of a reef community.

What do sponges, flamingos, and some whales have in common? All of them have built-in systems for straining food—plants or animals—from water. A sponge's body is filled with pores that filter out food. A flamingo has a set of strainers in its bill.

Tools of the Trade

The blue whale, largest animal ever known to have lived, has baleen—comblike plates that grow from its upper jaw. Many other kinds of whales have peglike teeth for catching prey. To eat, a blue whale simply swims with an open mouth through schools of tiny krill, animals that resemble shrimp. The whale's mouth fills with water and krill. Then it closes its mouth, straining the water out through the baleen. When only the krill remain, the whale swallows them. A blue whale's stomach holds about two tons of food at once. In a day, the whale may fill it with eight tons of krill!

To collect food, a blue whale uses its baleen; a chameleon uses its tongue; and a pelican uses its pouched bill. Some animals use tools from the environment to gather or eat food. A sea otter uses a rock as a tool. It puts the rock on its belly, then whacks a clam or other shellfish against it. The shell opens and the otter eats the food inside.

A chimp uses a stiff blade of (Continued on page 66)

STEPHEN KRASEMANN/NHPA

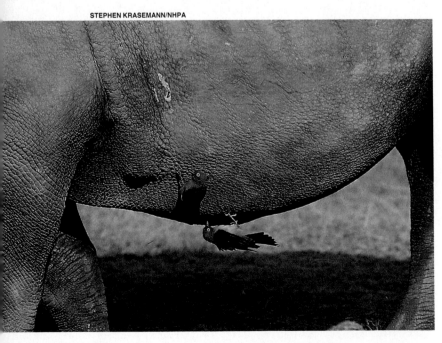

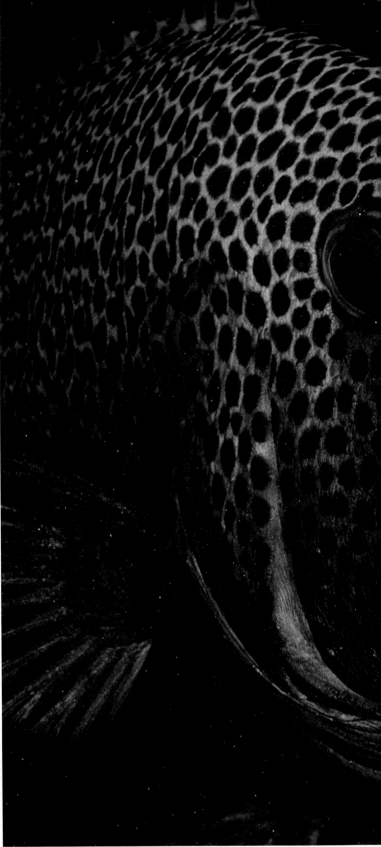

HOWARD HALL

Two red-billed oxpeckers (left), or tick birds, eat ticks and other parasites from the hide of a rhinoceros. They also warn the poor-sighted rhino of danger, with sharp calls. By grooming the rhino and by helping it "see," they get a feast in return. Such a give-and-take relationship is called symbiosis (sim-by-OH-sis).

The striped "tongue" on this spotted sweet lips fish (above) isn't a tongue at all. It's a small fish—a cleaner wrasse. A wrasse lives by nibbling parasites off larger fish, cleaning them. Its bold stripes and rocking swim advertise its services. Even predator fish line up quietly for cleaning. The wrasse may groom hundreds a day.

FRITZ PÖLKING

Wading on stiltlike legs, a lesser flamingo (above) lowers its bill to scoop up a meal of algae from a lake in Africa. Flamingo colors range from this bird's pale pink to a Caribbean flamingo's deep pink. The color depends on the kind of flamingo and on its diet. Pigments in the food of some birds help tint them pink.

To eat, a flamingo holds its bill upside down in the water (right) and uses its tongue to pump water in and out. Ridges rimming the bill strain out tiny plants and animals. The ridges of a lesser flamingo are very small. As the bird swishes its head from side to side, they trap microscopic plants, such as algae. Other flamingos have larger ridges that trap shrimps and snails.

LOIS SLOAN

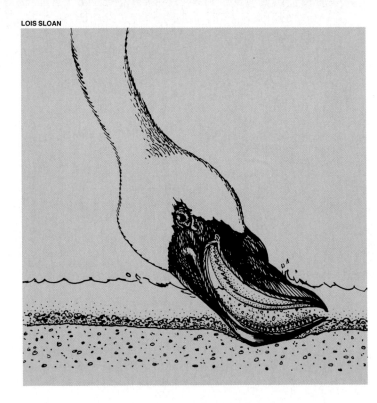

64

A pair of humpback whales surge to the surface (above), swallowing great mouthfuls of prey. These huge sea mammals eat some of the same kinds of food flamingos do—and in much the same way. The whales filter small creatures, krill, from the water. Comblike plates called baleen line their mouths. The whales gulp water, then force it out, catching the krill in the baleen.

Plates of baleen grow from a humpback's upper jaw (below). The plates are lined with bristles that strain food from the water. To eat, humpbacks may capture schools of krill by corralling them with nets of bubbles (right). Here, two whales swim in an upward spiral. Each spouts bubbles from two nostrils—blowholes— on top of its head. The bubbles trap the krill. Then all the whales swim through the food with open mouths.

Creature Feature

BARBARA L. GIBSON

(Continued from page 62) grass to extract termites from their nest in a mound of dirt. It pokes the grass into entrance holes the insects made. Inside, the termites bite the grass, trying to defend their home. Then the chimp pulls out the grass and eats the termites on it.

Other animals make their food. Honeybees, of course, make honey. In summer, they visit flowers and suck nectar into their honey sacs. Back in the hive, they empty the nectar into the mouths of other bees. The bees roll the nectar on their tongues, making water evaporate. Then they store the nectar in honeycomb, where it slowly thickens into honey.

Drink Up!

Eating is one requirement for living. Getting moisture is another. Most animals' bodies are 80 percent water. To maintain that percentage, they must constantly replace water lost through sweat, urination, and other bodily functions.

In deserts, where water is scarce, animals have amazing ways of surviving on very little liquid. In North Africa's Namib Desert, fog droplets collect on a beetle's back and drip into its mouth. Also desert natives, camels are expert water misers. They can drink 36 gallons in 10 minutes, then live for weeks on this liquid and on moisture they get from eating plants. Their body has ways of adapting: They sweat very little, their urine is concentrated, and their droppings are dry. Even their breath is dry. Most (Continued on page 70)

In dark ocean depths, a faint light sways. A fish swims toward it. Suddenly, GULP—the fish disappears into the gaping jaws of an anglerfish. What happened? The light came from the five-inch-long anglerfish (above). This fish has a spine growing from its head. The spine is tipped with a gland that holds bacteria. Oxygen combines with chemicals in the bacteria to produce light—and the light attracts prey. As a fish swims near, the anglerfish opens wide and swallows.

SMACK! A sea otter cracks open a clam against a rock it put on its chest (right). After eating the clam, the otter may tuck the rock in a pouch of skin under a foreleg, then dive for more food. Otters are one of the few animals known to use a tool—a rock. Observers saw one otter collect 54 shellfish in an hour and a half and whack them against a rock 2,000 times. JEFF FOOTT

Carrying a beakful, an acorn woodpecker (left) prepares to slip a winter's meal into a slot in its storage tree. The woodpecker chips thousands of small holes in a tree, then puts an acorn in each one. The bird will store food in the same tree winter after winter.

JIM CLARE © PARTRIDGE FILMS LTD/OXFORD SCIENTIFIC FILMS (LEFT)

WARLENE WEISSER/ARDEA LONDON (ABOVE)

When it comes to holes, an acorn woodpecker's tree (above) resembles a piece of Swiss cheese. Over time, 50,000 storage holes may be drilled in a tree by as many as 10 woodpeckers. In fall, the birds work together filling the holes with acorns and defending the supply from squirrels. The food must last through the winter.

DWIGHT R. KUHN

A busy bumblebee (above) sucks nectar from one of the hundred or more flowers it visits in a single day. The bee carries the nectar back to its hive in a honey sac in its body. Nectar from thousands of flowers will eventually produce a single teaspoonful of honey.

CAROL HUGHES/BRUCE COLEMAN LTD.

A leaf-cutter ant (above) lugs a leaf to its underground nest. Two smaller ants ride on the leaf, guarding the worker from attack by other insects. In the nest, ants will chew the leaf into a paste and spread it into a "garden." A kind of fungus resembling mushrooms will grow there, providing food for the entire ant colony.

(Continued from page 66) animals exhale moist air. A camel's nostrils remove moisture as the camel breathes out, then add it to the dry air the camel breathes in.

Eating and drinking are essential functions of life. But they're useless if an animal doesn't breathe. Breathing in supplies vital oxygen to every part of an animal's body. Breathing out expels carbon dioxide and other wastes. On land, mammals, birds, and reptiles breathe with lungs. In water, fish and other creatures use respiratory systems such as gills for getting oxygen from the water. When a mammal lives in water and a fish ventures onto dry land, amazing things happen.

Deep Breathers

The sperm whale is the deepest recorded diver. This mammal can descend a mile, staying under for an hour. First it takes many breaths. The oxygen combines with substances in the whale's body so it can be used slowly. Diving, the whale's heartbeat slows and the blood flow to its muscles decreases. This makes the oxygen last a long time.

Most fish out of water have been caught for dinner. The mudskipper, however, climbs out to find dinner. With powerful leglike fins, it scoots up onto a muddy bank, looking for tiny crabs. As it emerges, it soaks its gills with water. On land, the moist gills provide the fish with oxygen. The mudskipper can stay out for hours at a time. It eats, maintains water, and breathes—all basic functions of life. And it takes a tour of the animal kingdom's dry side, besides.

SLUURP. A thirsty giraffe takes a long drink (above). The water must travel six feet or more—the length of an adult's neck. Giraffes get enough moisture from eating leaves. But when water is near, a giraffe spreads its forelegs, bends its knees, and lowers its head. Valves in its neck veins slow the flow of blood to its head so that when it straightens up, it won't get dizzy.

An elephant (above) fills its trunk and—SPLASH! It's bath time. The trunk also helps the elephant drink, eat, and breathe. To drink, the elephant sucks up a gallon of water, then squirts it into its mouth. To eat, it plucks leaves with the trunk's flexible tip and tucks them into its mouth. Finally, it breathes through nostrils in its trunk—actually an elongated nose and upper lip.

Often called ships of the desert, camels (left) stride across the waterless terrain. Camels can survive weeks without a drink. They don't store water in their humps, an old theory. Instead, their body functions help them conserve liquid. They exhale dry air, they rarely sweat, and their droppings are dry. They can restock quickly, too, drinking 36 gallons in 10 minutes.

71

WHOOSH! As a humpback whale exhales, it blows water into the air (above). Like all other mammals, a whale has lungs and breathes air. Depending on its kind, it has one or two blowholes for breathing. After taking several deep breaths, some whales can stay submerged an hour. Their bodies make the oxygen last.

Many animals store food. The European water spider (above) stores air as well. On an underwater plant, the spider spins a tightly woven web. Then the spider swims to the surface, traps an air bubble, and carries it back to the web. Once the web is filled with air, the spider uses it as a hunting base.

Fish out of water, a mudskipper (right) climbs a branch using its leglike fins. All fish get oxygen from water through gills. If the gills dry out, a fish suffocates. As a mudskipper emerges, it soaks its gills with water. On land, the gills stay safely moist, and the fish breathes the oxygen.

From its perch on a rock underwater, a marine iguana looks around for a meal. The world's only seagoing lizards, marine iguanas live mostly on land, but they slip into water to eat algae. Such an iguana can dive 45 feet and stay under for half an hour. While it is holding its breath, its heartbeat slows. This conserves oxygen.
HOWARD HALL

74

5
On Guard!

B-E-W-A-R-E. The long, slender spines on this lionfish spell just that. The delicately fringed creature appears to flutter lazily over a coral reef. But it is always on guard. If a fish—or a diver—swims too near, the intruder will get a jab from a spine filled with poison.

When it comes to built-in weapons of defense, few animals are as well equipped as the lionfish. But almost every animal has at least one way of defending itself against enemies. Depending on the animal and its armor, there are many tactics: Run! Hide! Startle! Distract! Fight! The next pages will feature these and other ways that animals stay on guard.

JEFFREY L. ROTMAN

To survive, all animals must eat. They must also avoid being eaten. This is no easy task. Underwater, small fish are chased by larger fish. On land, gazelles are stalked by lions. In the air, insects are snatched up by bats and by birds. The list goes on and on.

To defend themselves, animals use many different means, depending on their body structures and on what they have learned. Some, like the lionfish, fight an enemy by using poison. Others hide by blending with their surroundings. Some animals trick their way out of trouble. This kind of defense may be learned from their parents, or it may be instinctive. The most common defense is instinctive: To run away—fast. Animals with sophisticated defense mechanisms often run first, using other methods only if cornered.

Some animals avoid predators by being team players. They live in groups and cooperate in group defense. Musk-oxen, for example, are social animals that live in herds. When threatened by a wolf pack, these huge creatures quickly form a protective barrier around their young. They stand with their horns pointing outward. If the pack comes too close, the oxen will charge. Prairie dogs, rodents of

LEN RUE, JR.

Buddy system. Meerkats (left) scan the sky for danger, possibly a hungry hawk. These squirrel-size animals live in desert regions in southern Africa. Their families are tightly knit. Members share food, care of the young, and guard duty. As some eat insects or lizards, others stand guard. If there is danger, the sentries give shrill cries, sending the group racing to the burrow.

DAVID MACDONALD/OXFORD SCIENTIFIC FILMS

Circle up! Musk-oxen in Alaska stand in a ring around their calves (right), defending the young from enemies such as wolves. Their sharp, curved horns form a protective shield that most attackers can't penetrate. If enemies persist, the oxen may charge them.

Hightailing it, a white-tailed deer (above) dashes down a bank. By lifting its tail to show the white underside, it alerts other deer to danger. They all bound away, sometimes reaching speeds of 30 miles an hour. Once the deer have run to safety—perhaps in a dense grove of trees—they may watch quietly for enemies. Their brown coats blend with forest colors, helping to hide them.

North American grasslands, also cooperate in groups. When the animals look for food outside their burrows, they keep watch. If one sees a coyote or other enemy, it cries a shrill warning. All the prairie dogs scoot underground.

Troops of baboons live on the plains of East Africa. These monkeys move slowly through tall grasses, eating vegetation. Together, they keep a sharp lookout for predators. If one baboon spots a slinking leopard or a lion, it shrieks loudly, and all the baboons try to flee. Sometimes, however, the monkeys are cornered. Then, the males will charge the enemy, barking furiously. Often, the predator gives up. But if it persists, the baboons will close in and attack. Working together, they usually drive the enemy away—or even kill it.

Playing Tricks

Defense tactics used by musk-oxen and baboons prove that there is safety in numbers. The animals' size and strength are a big help, too. A killdeer, a dove-size bird that lives in North America, does not have the advantage of group cooperation—or of size. To protect itself and its young, the killdeer plays tricks.

Killdeers make nests on the ground. Together, male and female incubate their eggs. While sitting on the nest, one parent may spot a predator. Immediately, the bird goes into action. It limps away from the nest, holding one wing away from its body, as if broken. The predator follows. The

I'm injured! A killdeer (above) seems to say just that as it lurches across the ground. It drags one wing as if it were broken. The broken-wing display distracts a coyote from the bird's nest on the ground (right). The coyote follows the killdeer, which appears to offer an easy meal. When the bird has lured the enemy away, it quickly flies back to its nest to guard it.

The tail of an anole (uh-KNOW-lee), a kind of lizard, sometimes tells this tale: The lizard has had a narrow escape. If an enemy bites the tail, it breaks off easily. Muscles tighten around the break and prevent bleeding. The detached tail continues wiggling, distracting the predator (below) while the lizard flees. Like the one at right, the escaped anole soon grows a new tail.

JAMES H. ROBINSON

LOIS SLOAN (ABOVE AND BELOW)

81

JIM FRAZIER/MANTIS WILDLIFE

A frilled lizard (left) keeps very still, camouflaged against a branch. If an enemy spots it and comes too close, the lizard will hiss loudly, puffing up with air. It will flip up a collar, or frill, around its neck . . .

. . . as this lizard does (below). The alarming display startles a predator by making the lizard appear much larger—too large to eat. If the display doesn't discourage the enemy—perhaps a dog or a snake—the lizard will turn and run away at top speed.

killdeer continues to flutter across the ground, keeping just out of the predator's reach. When the bird has led the predator a safe distance from the nest, it takes off and flies home.

Other tricksters put off predators by putting on instant disguises. Here's an example: A dog chases a cat into a corner. Hissing and snarling, the cat arches its back and raises its fur. The dog crouches and creeps away. Noise and a sudden change in appearance have made the cat look larger than it really is, causing its enemy to back down. Many other animals use similar tactics to startle predators.

The Australian frilled lizard puffs up its body with air and snaps open a big, colorful collar of skin around its neck. It opens its mouth wide and hisses.

A porcupine fish really puffs up. When an enemy comes near, the fish gulps in water, expanding to three times its normal size. As it fills out, sharp spines that lie flat against its body pop out. The fish turns as prickly as a porcupine. Most enemies don't stay for dinner.

An animal's sudden transformation may not always frighten a predator. But the display may (Continued on page 85)

(Continued from page 82) startle the enemy long enough for the animal to escape. The frilled lizard's bluff, for instance, may not be enough. If an enemy stands its ground, the lizard rears up on its strong hind legs and runs to safety.

Often, staying safe means staying out of sight. Some animals, such as moles and chipmunks, dig deep underground burrows that keep them far from the claws and jaws of predators. The caterpillar of the skipper butterfly makes a cover that hides it. It folds a piece of a leaf over itself, then binds the piece to the rest of the leaf using silken threads spun by its body. Surrounded by other leaves, the cover is camouflaged. In it, the caterpillar stays safe from birds.

The Untouchables

Other animals have body parts that help them disappear. A turtle tucks its legs under its protective shell and pulls its head inside. Made of a hard, bony substance, the shell is so tough that most enemies can't bite through it. The armadillo lizard's back and tail are protected by scaly plates. When enemies go after its soft belly, the lizard flips on its back and pulls its tail up, tucking it between its jaws. The animal becomes a scaly ring, its belly protected by its back.

Some animals defend themselves by reminding enemies that they are poisonous if eaten. Such animals have colorful bodies, or they give off foul odors, or both. The color and smell warn of poison in their bodies.

Fire-bellied toads, which live in southeastern Asia, have deadly poisons in their skin. They alert enemies to the poisons by showing off bright patterns on their undersides. When an enemy approaches, such a toad arches its back and lifts up its legs, revealing its pattern. One look is often enough to send the enemy elsewhere for food.

Animals with an appetite for butterflies steer clear of monarchs. These insects feed on poison-filled milkweed plants and absorb the poison into their systems. By simply fluttering their brilliant orange-and-black wings, they tell enemies to leave them alone. (Continued on page 89)

It's open house for this skipper caterpillar (above). The photographer gently peeled open its nest to uncover the animal inside. The caterpillar makes a nest that hides it from birds. It folds a piece of a leaf over itself, then sews the leaf shut with silk strands from its body.

The finished home (above) resembles a sleeping bag. Nestled in it, the skipper caterpillar is hard to detect. It lives inside for three months. For food, it eats the leafy home. The caterpillar does not chew out a hole big enough to give itself away. It nibbles a little here and a little there, giving the leaf a lacy look.

BOO! Like a Halloween goblin, a female praying mantis (left) rears up on her hind legs, raises her forelegs, and extends her wings. Atop a case filled with her eggs, she presents an alarming display to enemies, often birds and monkeys. Dark dots on her upper body resemble eyes and help to further confuse attackers.

EDWARD S. ROSS (ALL)

85

ANTHONY BANNISTER/ NHPA

Don't touch me! When threatened, a milkweed grasshopper (above) gives off a foul-smelling foam. The foam and the insect's bright colors tell enemies such as birds that the grasshopper is dangerous. As it eats poisonous milkweed plants, its body absorbs the poison. Predators that bite the insect are in big trouble.

The caterpillar of the swallowtail butterfly might be called a real stinker (below). If approached by a wasp or a fly, the caterpillar lifts its head and extends a pinkish, Y-shaped gland from it. The gland produces a bad smell, which often sends predators fleeing.

DENSEY CLYNE/MANTIS WILDLIFE

Creature Feature

One step closer, and I'll fire! Stamping its feet and raising its tail, a skunk (right) warns an intruder to stay away. If the intruder ignores the signals—SWOOSH—the skunk lets out a foul-smelling spray from glands under its tail. The spray burns and even blinds temporarily. The odor hangs on for days.

disc

BARBARA L. GIBSON

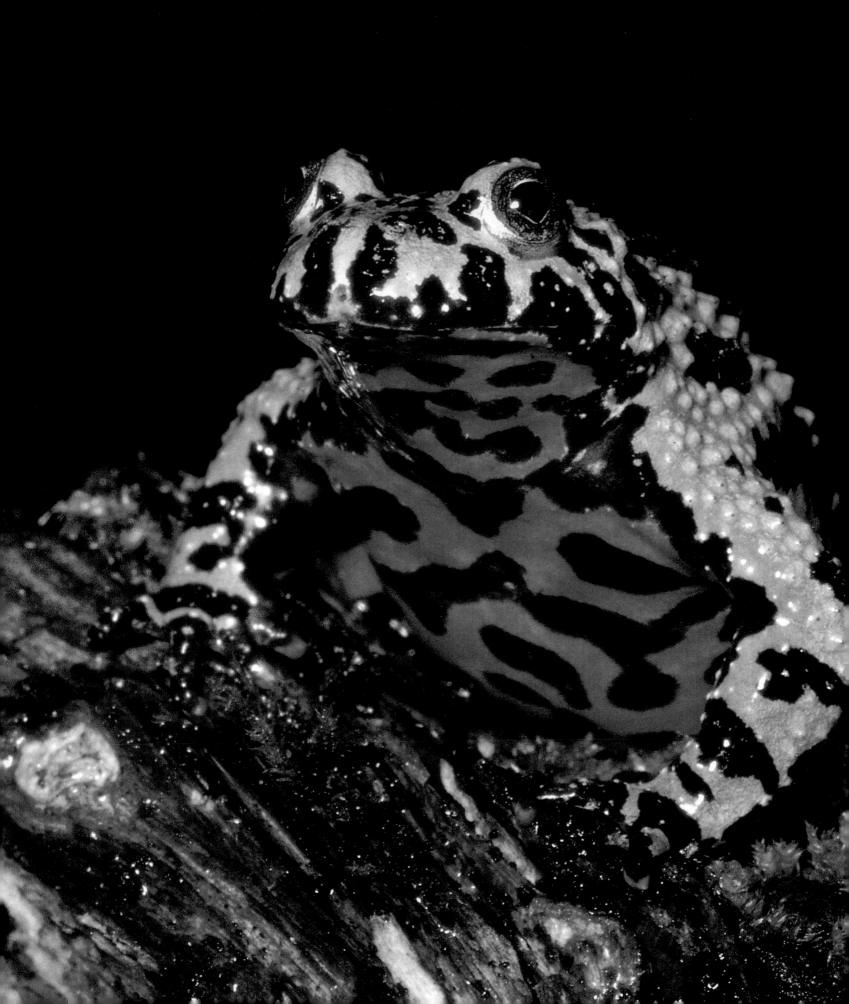

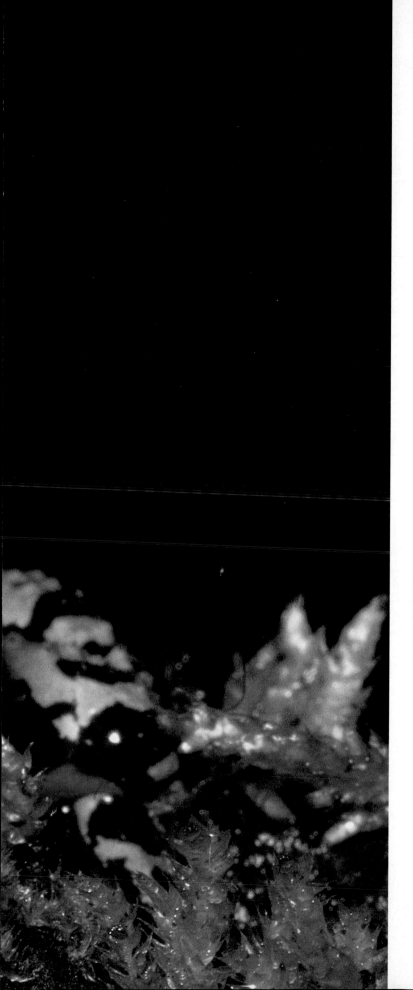

(Continued from page 85) When a skunk stamps its feet and waves its black-and-white-striped tail, a predator is in for a nasty surprise. Glands under the skunk's tail are about to spray a burning, foul-smelling liquid that may temporarily blind the enemy—and stay in its coat for days.

Defense may not always mean taking action. Sometimes sitting still is enough to discourage a predator. Imagine this: In a tropical forest, a small bird hops from leaf to leaf, looking for food. It passes right by a leaf weighed down with another bird's dropping and moves on. For a moment, all is quiet. Suddenly—the dropping stirs! It stands up, then crawls away on eight spidery legs.

The "dropping" is a bolas spider. To avoid enemies, it sits on a leaf and pulls its legs up beneath it. Then its shape and color make it look so unappetizing that predators pass it up. It is one of many small animals that can hide because they resemble parts of their environment. One insect, a mantis, stands on an orchid and looks like a petal. A thorn bug, with its thorn-shaped body, appears to grow from the twig it sits on. A grasshopper crouching in a field resembles a blade of

Colorful and deadly, a fire-bellied toad (left) rests on a log. The toad's undersides are reddish from eating food that has carotene, a substance that makes carrots orange. The color tells snakes and birds that the toad's skin holds poisons. When threatened, the toad displays the color by arching its back and lifting its legs.

MICHAEL FOGDEN (LEFT)

CAROL HUGHES (ABOVE)

To hungry animals, two peas in a pod would taste much better than these two poison-arrow frogs posed in a mushroom (above). Like the fire-bellied toad, these South American frogs have a reddish color that tells enemies their skins secrete powerful poisons. Local Indians apply the poisons to the tips of hunting arrows.

*These lumps on a log (above) are actually a tawny
frogmouth bird and her chick resting on a fallen tree.
Natives of Australia, such birds are camouflage artists.
The color of bark, a frogmouth stays hidden from
hawks during the day because it blends with the tree it
sits on. At night, the bird eats insects from the ground.*

*Would the real thorn please stand up? A treehopper
called a thorn bug (right) perches near a thorn on a
twig. The insect gets its nickname from its spiky upper
body. The spike helps guard it from enemies. Even if a
bird can distinguish between a thorn and a thorn bug,
it may still avoid eating such a prickly looking meal.*

dry grass. Against their matching backgrounds, these animals disappear from view.

One African spider uses an opposite tactic in its defense. Instead of looking like something else, it makes something else that looks like *it*. Using silk from its body, it spins fake spiders in its web. Then it sits in the center. Birds zoom in on the fakes and get a beakful of web, not juicy spider.

Staying on guard means staying alive. It is essential to life—as are traveling, communicating, raising babies, and taking in nourishment. To perform these functions, each animal has its own methods, from acrobatics to aquatics. How can an observer see some? A trip around the world is one way. Another way is simply to *look* around. In a quiet neighborhood, a squirrel walks a tightrope—a telephone wire—for hundreds of feet without a slip. In a city park, a male pigeon courts a female in a ritual that includes bowing and feeding her seeds. In a home aquarium, a male Siamese fighting fish builds a nest of bubbles for its young. On a side street, a cat pounces on a mouse at lightning speed. Everywhere, every second, animals do things that are—amazing!

ANIMALS ANIMALS/JOHN GERLACH

The crab spider (above) has different wardrobes for different occasions. If it climbs onto a white flower, it slowly takes on a white color. If it moves to a yellow flower, it turns yellow. The spider gets its name from the way it moves. It scuttles sideways, as a crab does.

Here, a crab spider makes a perfect match for its yellow perch (below). Its ability to blend with its surroundings helps it avoid hungry birds. When the spider wants to eat, it hides beneath a petal. There it can ambush insects that land on the flower.

ANIMALS ANIMALS/GEORGE K. BRYCE

STEPHEN J. KRASEMANN/DRK PHOTO

Now it's a caterpillar, now it's a . . . snake? The caterpillar of a sphinx moth (above) masquerades as a snake if trouble comes its way. It inflates its head and part of its body into a triangular shape, like a serpent's. Fake eyes bulge out. The bluff may frighten enemies.

Three anoles sharing a slender branch show the lizards' range of coloration—from greens to browns. They turn the different shades as they are affected by temperature, light, and stress—such as approaching enemies. When they are cold, in the dark, or afraid, they turn brown. When they are warm, in bright light, or feeling safe, they turn green. The colors help them blend in with the environment to hide from birds or snakes.

JAMES H. ROBINSON

Index

ADDITIONAL READING

Readers may want to check issues of *WORLD* magazine, the *National Geographic Index,* or a public library for related articles and to refer to the following books and periodicals. ("A" indicates material at the adult level.)

PERIODICALS: International Wildlife (A), *National Wildlife* (A), *Ranger Rick,* all The National Wildlife Federation. *Natural History,* American Museum of Natural History (A). *Smithsonian,* Smithsonian Associates (A).

BOOKS: Bright, Michael, *Animal Language,* BBC, 1984 (A). Foy, Sally, *The Grand Design: Form and Color in Animals,* J.M. Dent & Sons Ltd., 1982 (A). C.A.W., *Wild Cats of the World,* Taplinger Publishing Company, 1975. Jackson, M.H., *Galapagos: A Natural History Guide,* The University of Calgary Press, 1985 (A). King, Judith E., *Seals of the World,* British Museum, l983. MacClintock, Dorcas, *A Natural History of Giraffes,* Charles Scribner's Sons, 1973. Mattison, Chris, *Frogs and Toads of the World,* Facts On File Publishers, 1987 (A). Milne, Lorus, and Margery, *A Time to be Born,* Sierra Club Books, 1982. Preston-Mafham, Rod and Ken, *Spiders of the World,* Blandford Press, 1984 (A). Robinson, David, *Living Wild: The Secrets of Animal Survival,* The National Wildlife Federation, 1980 (A). Street, Philip, *Animal Reproduction,* Taplinger Publishing Company, 1974. Ward, Peter, *Color For Survival,* Orbis Publications, Inc., 1979. Watson, Lyall, *Sea Guide to Whales of the World,* E.P. Dutton, 1981 (A). Welty, Joel, *The Life of Birds,* Saunders College Publishing, 1982 (A). Wilson, Roberta, and James Q., *Watching Fishes: Life and Behavior on Coral Reefs,* Harper & Row, 1985 (A). Wootton, Anthony, *Insects of the World,* Facts On File Publications, 1984 (A). Wyllie, Ian, *The Cuckoo,* Universe Books, 1981 (A).

BOOKS BY THE NATIONAL GEOGRAPHIC SOCIETY: The Amazing Animals of Australia, 1984. *Animal Architects,* 1987. *Dolphins: Our Friends in the Sea,* 1986. *Field Guide to the Birds of North America,* 1983 (A). *How Animals Behave: A New Look at Wildlife,* 1984. *Geo-Whiz!,* 1988. *How Animals Talk,* 1987. *The Marvels of Animal Behavior,* 1972 (A). *The Mysterious Undersea World,* 1980. *Wild Animals of North America,* 1979 (A). *The Wonder of Birds,* 1983 (A).

CONSULTANTS

Fiona Sunquist, *Chief Consultant*
Stanley Fagen, Ph.D., *Consulting Psychologist*
Frank J. Sanford, *Reading Consultant*

The Special Publications and School Services Division is grateful to the individuals cited here for their generous assistance:
   C. Michael Bailey, National Aquarium; May R. Berenbaum, University of Illinois; Claud Bramblett, University of Texas; James L. Castner, University of Florida; Valerie Chase, National Aquarium in Baltimore; Scott Eckert, University of Georgia; Alfred L. Gardner, U. S. Fish and Wildlife Service; John L. Hoogland, University of Maryland, Center for Environmental and Estuarine Studies; Thomas A. Jenssen, Virginia Polytechnic Institute and State University; David W. Macdonald, University of Oxford; Douglass R. Miller, David A. Nickle, Systematic Entomology Laboratory, U. S. Department of Agriculture; David L. Pawson, Smithsonian Institution; Craig Phillips, Silver Spring, Maryland; Bruce Robison, Monterey Bay Aquarium Research Institute; Edward S. Ross, Curator of Entomology, California Academy of Sciences; Wendell Swank, Texas A & M University; Merlin D. Tuttle, Bat Conservation International; George E. Watson, St. Albans School, Washington, D. C.

Composition for THE AMAZING THINGS ANIMALS DO by the Typographic section of National Geographic Production Services, Pre-Press Division. Printed and bound by R.R. Donnelley & Sons Co., Chicago, Illinois. Color separations by Lanman–Progressive Co., Washington, D. C.; Lincoln Graphics, Inc., Cherry Hill, N.J.; and Graphic Art Service, Nashville, Tenn. Cover printed by Federated Lithographers–Printers, Inc., Providence, R.I. Teacher's Guide printed by McCollum Press, Inc., Rockville, Md.

Library of Congress CIP Data
McGrath, Susan, 1955-
   The amazing things animals do.
   (Books for world explorers)
   Bibliography: p.
   Includes index.
   Summary: Examines how different animals move, communicate, raise their young, take in nourishment, and defend themselves.
   1. Animal behavior—Juvenile literature.   2. Animals—Juvenile literature.
   [1. Animals—Habits and behavior]   I. Title.   II. Series.
   QL751.5.M39 1989   591.5'1   89-9428
      ISBN 0–87044–704–1
      ISBN 0–87044–709–2 (lib. bdg.)

THE AMAZING THINGS ANIMALS DO

PUBLISHED BY
THE NATIONAL GEOGRAPHIC SOCIETY
WASHINGTON, D. C.

Gilbert M. Grosvenor, *President and Chairman of the Board*
Melvin M. Payne, Thomas W. McKnew, *Chairmen Emeritus*
Owen R. Anderson, *Executive Vice President*
Robert L. Breeden, *Senior Vice President*
Publications and Educational Media

PREPARED BY THE SPECIAL PUBLICATIONS AND SCHOOL SERVICES DIVISION
Donald J. Crump, *Director*
Philip B. Silcott, *Associate Director*
Bonnie S. Lawrence, *Assistant Director*

BOOKS FOR WORLD EXPLORERS
Pat Robbins, *Editor*
Ralph Gray, *Editor Emeritus*
Ursula Perrin Vosseler, *Art Director*
Margaret McKelway, *Associate Editor*
Larry Nighswander, *Illustrations Editor*

STAFF FOR *THE AMAZING THINGS ANIMALS DO*
M. Barbara Brownell, *Managing Editor*
Veronica J. Morrison, *Illustrations Editor*
Drayton Hawkins, *Art Director*
Bruce G. Norfleet, *Researcher/Writer*
Catherine D. Hughes, *Project Outline*
Sheila M. Green, *Senior Researcher*
Kathryn N. Adams, Sandra F. Lotterman, Nancy J. White
Editorial Assistants
Janet A. Dustin, Jennie H. Proctor, *Illustrations Assistants*

ENGRAVING, PRINTING, AND PRODUCT MANUFACTURE: Gregory Storer, George J. Zeller, *Managers, Manufacturing and Quality Management;* David V. Showers, *Production Manager;* Lewis R. Bassford, *Production Project Manager;* Kathie Cirucci, Timothy H. Ewing, *Senior Production Assistants;* Kevin Heubusch, *Production Assistant;* Carol R. Curtis, *Senior Production Staff Assistant*

STAFF ASSISTANTS: Aimée L. Brown, Catherine G. Cruz, Marisa Farabelli, Mary Elizabeth House, Rebecca A. Hutton, Karen Katz, Lisa A. LaFuria, Eliza C. Morton, Dru Stancampiano

MARKET RESEARCH: Joseph S. Fowler, Carrla L. Holmes, Marla Lewis, Joseph Roccanova, Donna R. Schoeller, Marsha Sussman, Judy T. Guerrieri

INDEX: Michael G. Young